GIVE UP

LIFE'S AN ADVENTURE FOR MOST...
A CONCUSSION FOR YOU.

PAUL KOEHORST & IVOR JONES

Ulysses Press

Published in the U.S. by:
ULYSSES PRESS
P.O. Box 3440
Berkeley, CA 94703
www.ulyssespress.com

ISBN 978-1-56975-740-6
Library of Congress Control Number: 2009941119

Printed in the United States by Bang Printing

10 9 8 7 6 5 4 3 2

Acquisitions: Nick Denton-Brown
Proofreaders: Lauren Harrison, Lily Chou
Production: Judith Metzener
Cover design: what!design @ whatweb.com
Cover photo: ©istockphoto.com/AhavatHaEmet

Distributed by Publishers Group West

TABLE OF CONTENTS

SYNERGY

THE STRENGTH OF THE TEAM IS IN EACH MEMBER.
THE STRENGTH OF EACH MEMBER IS IN THE TEAM.
LONG STORY SHORT: YOU'RE HOLDING EVERYONE BACK.

DISCOVERY

THE LONGEST JOURNEY BEGINS WITH A SINGLE STEP. . .
PREFERABLY ONTO AN AIRPLANE.

MISTAKES

SOMETIMES THEY *ARE* A MATTER OF LIFE AND DEATH.

CHEATING

YOU'RE NEVER TOO YOUNG TO START.

PROFESSIONALISM

DIVERSITY

DIFFERENT COLORS. DIFFERENT SIZES.
DIFFERENT REASONS WE ALL HATE WENDY FROM ACCOUNTING

TRUST

**BE CAREFUL WHO YOU TRUST;
YOU COULD CATCH A LOT WORSE THAN A LITTLE KID.**

DEFEAT

You May Not Have Won, but Nothing Beats a Good Excuse

FRIENDSHIP

BECAUSE SHE HASN'T LET YOU FUCK HER YET

INSPIRE

**BE THE ROCK SOMEONE'S SUCCESS IS FOUNDED UPON,
THE FIRE IN THEIR EYES, THE WIND THAT PUSHES THEM TO THE TOP—JUST IN
CASE SOMEDAY YOU NEED TO HIT THEM UP FOR MONEY.**

DECISIONS

GOOD DECISIONS COME FROM EXPERIENCE. EXPERIENCE COMES FROM BAD DECISIONS. BAD DECISIONS COME FROM TEQUILA.

SUCCESS

**FAILURE IS NOT AN OPTION,
BUT A CAREER IN FAST FOOD DEFINITELY IS.**

TRUST

A Faithful Companion Is a Sure Anchor. . .
Unless Your Anchor Is a Cheap Bastard Who Buys
Bargain-bin Climbing Rope.

TEAMWORK

NEVER UNDERESTIMATE THE PERSONAL SATISFACTION
OF HAVING PLENTY OF OTHERS TO BLAME FOR YOUR OWN MISTAKES

YOUR EX

SLEEPING WITH YOUR EX IS LIKE USING AN OLD TUBE OF TOOTHPASTE: YOU CAN ALWAYS SQUEEZE ONE MORE OUT.

BLUETOOTHS

THANKS FOR LETTING US KNOW, FROM A SAFE DISTANCE, THAT YOU'RE A DOUCHE BAG.

NETWORKING

IT'S NOT *WHAT* YOU KNOW, IT'S *WHO* YOU KNOW. SO YOU'D BETTER START KISSING SOME ASS.

FUTILITY

**WHAT DO YOU EXPECT TO ACHIEVE
WHEN YOU CAN'T EVEN CONQUER LIFE'S BUNNY SLOPES?**

FATHERHOOD

CUT THE BULLSHIT... HE ALREADY KNOWS WHERE YOU HIDE YOUR PO

ACTION

YOU CAN'T MAKE AN OMELET WITHOUT BREAKING A FEW EGGS. . .
AND I SUPPOSE YOU THINK THAT'S FINE, YOU UNBORN BABY CHICKEN KILLER

GOALS

THE ONLY THING STOPPING YOU IS YOU
(AND NOT IN A GOOD WAY).

DRINKING

IT'S ALL FUN AND GAMES . . .
TILL YOU WAKE UP NEXT TO A PENGUIN.

MONEY

Why Work for It when You Can Marry It?

AMBITION

**LIKE A SIREN'S SONG, DRAWING YOU EVER CLOSER
TO THE JAGGED ROCKS OF LIFE'S DISAPPOINTMENTS**

INTEGRITY

**. . . IS SHOWN WHEN NO ONE IS LOOKING.
(SO WATCH OUT FOR NANNY CAMS.)**

OPTIMISM

THE OPTIMIST SEES THE ROSE AND NOT THE THORNS.
THE PESSIMIST SEES THE THORNS AND NOT THE ROSE.
THE BLIND MAN THINKS HIS BLOOD SMELLS NICE.

LAZINESS

IF IT FEELS SO RIGHT, HOW CAN IT BE WRONG?

DO IT

**IN LIFE, IT PAYS TO TRY YOUR HAND AT EVERYTHING YOU CAN—
HOW ELSE WILL YOU DISCOVER ALL THE THINGS YOU SUCK AT?**

HONESTY

WE'D BE LYING IF WE SAID IT WAS ALWAYS THE BEST POLICY.

SLACKING OFF

THOSE WHO ARE CUTE AND CUDDLY CAN GET AWAY WITH ANYTHING.

DISAPPOINTMENT

JUST BECAUSE HE'S NOT THE NEXT TIGER WOODS . . .
DOESN'T MEAN ANOTHER FAMILY WON'T TAKE HIM OFF YOUR HANDS

EXTREME

Go for It—You Only Have One Chance at Life. Then Again, There's Any Number of Dumb Ways to Get Yourself Killed.

TATTOOS

TO YOU IT SAYS "STRENGTH." TO ANYONE WHO ACTUALLY SPEAKS
CHINESE, IT SAYS "GOAT FUCKER."

OPPORTUNITY

ANOTHER DAY, ANOTHER CHANCE TO JUST SKATE BY.

FAILURE

FINALLY SOMETHING YOU'RE GOOD AT.

RELATIONSHIPS

IF IT IS TO BE, IT IS UP TO ME. BUT IF IT'S UP TO HER, I'M SCREWED FOR SURE.

ABCS

OF COURSE I KNOW MY FUCKING ABCS... ALWAYS BE CLOSING

FACEBOOK

HUMILITY

PATRIOTISM.

LIFE, LIBERTY AND THE FREEDOM TO HUMILIATE YOUR PETS.

HOPELESS

YOU CAN'T STOP THE WAVES, BUT YOU CAN LEARN TO SURF . . .
WELL, MAYBE NOT YOU.

LOVE

THERE'S NO ACCOUNTING FOR TASTE.

DESTINY

**THE BEST WAY TO PREDICT YOUR FUTURE IS TO CREATE IT . . .
SO KEEP PADDING YOUR RESUME.**

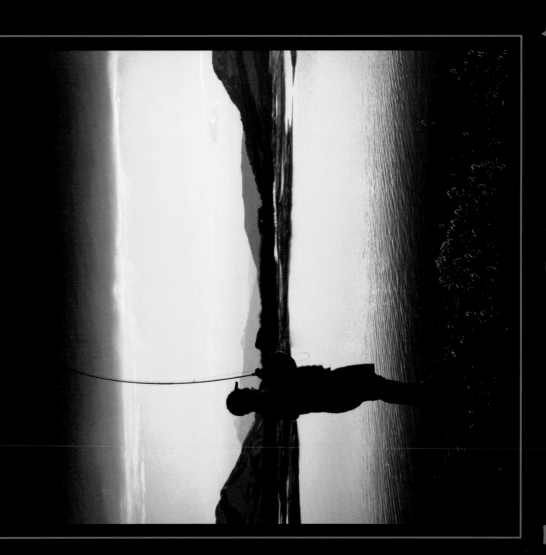

UNEMPLOYMENT

THE PAY MIGHT SUCK, BUT YOU CAN'T BEAT THE HOURS.

PROTECTED PLACE　保 护 区

NO
ADMITTANCE
TO UNAUTHORISED
PERSONS

闲 人 免 进

DI LARANG MASOK
JIKA TIADA
KEBENARAN

உத்தரவின்றி
உள்ளே
பிரவேசிக்க
கூடாது

TEMPAT LARANGAN　பாதுகாப்பு உள்ள இடம்

RULES

RULES ARE MADE TO BE BROKEN. BUT YOU GO FIRST.

GETTING FIRED

On the Bright Side, It Might Get You Laid.

PANHANDLERS

FINALLY A CHARITY YOU CAN GET BEHIND: BOOZE.

SPORTS CARS

**WHEN PILLS, PUMPS AND MEDICAL PROCEDURES
ARE UNABLE TO SOLVE YOUR LITTLE PROBLEM**

FREELOADING

ALL THE GLORY, HALF THE EFFORT.

DIETING

WHEN THE COOKIE'S THE SIZE OF YOUR HEAD,
DO YOU REALLY NEED TO ASK HOW MANY "POINTS"

SEARCH ENGINES

THEY ONLY WORK IF YOU'RE SPECIFIC.

SUCCESS

10% Inspiration, 90% Perspiration*.

= 50% Loan from Grandparents, 20% Insider Trading, 10% Government Bailout, 10% Dumb Luck)

ATTITUDE

THE PESSIMIST WORRIES ABOUT THE WEATHER. THE OPTIMIST EXPECTS THE STORM TO PASS. THE CAPTAIN IS A DRUNK AND YOU'RE ALL GOING TO DROWN ANYWAY.

S-T-R-A-T-E-G-Y

STRIVING TOGETHER RAISING ATTITUDES TOTALLY EVERYDAY. . . GRAVY. . . YACHTS.

COURAGE

It Comes Easier if You Have Health Insurance

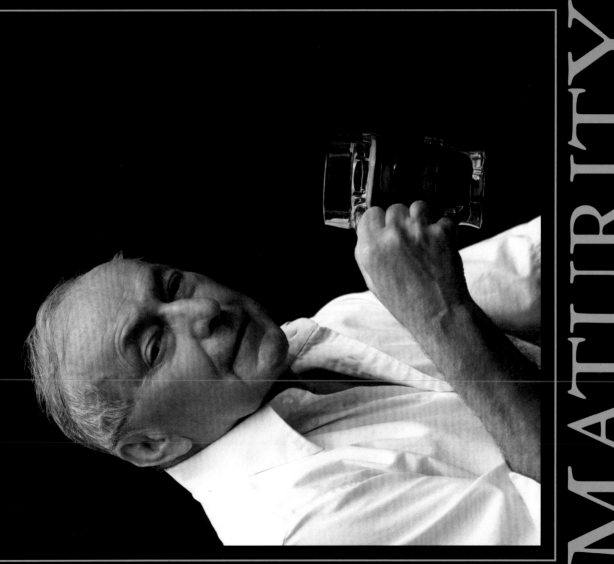

MATURITY

YOU MIGHT HAVE A FEW YEARS ON THE REST OF US, OLD MAN . . . BUT YOU'RE STILL FULL OF SHIT.

DUCT TAPE

THE HALF-ASSED WAY TO KIND OF FIX THINGS FOR OVER 60 YEARS.

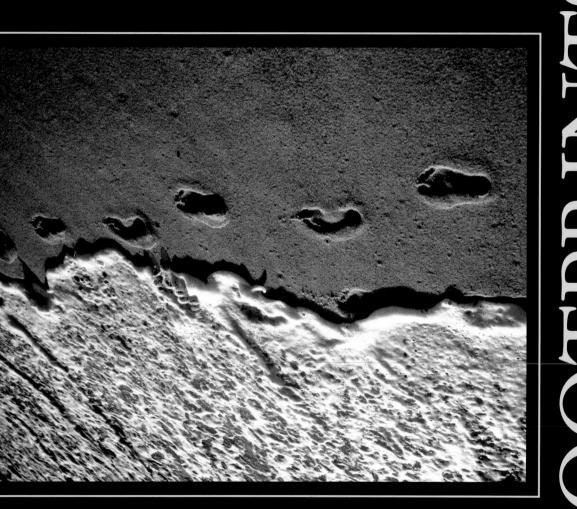

FOOTPRINTS

LORD, WHY DID YOU LEAVE ME TO WALK ALONE?
"SERIOUSLY, THE BITCH DUMPED YOU . . . DO YOU KNOW
HOW MANY PRAYERS I GET FROM KIDS WITH CANCER?"

CHAIN REACTION

IF A BUTTERFLY FLAPPING ITS WINGS IN AFRICA CAN CAUSE A TYPHOON IN CHINA, I DON'T EVEN WANT TO KNOW WHAT KIND OF DAMAGE A GASSY HIPPO COULD DO.

CUBICLES

JUST THINK OF IT AS AN OFFICE WITH A SUNROOF.

WISDOM

THAT ONE MAGICAL AND UNREPEATABLE TIME WHEN SOMEHOW YOUR BULLSHIT ACTUALLY MADE SENSE.

MOTORCYCLES

127-Inch V-Twin Engine, 6-speed Tranny, Single-sided Swingarm, 115 Pounds of Foot Torque and 1 Mean Midlife Crisis.

LEADERSHIP

**LEADERS ARE NOT BORN,
THEY ARE FORGED AT SEMINARS IN HOTELS BY THE AIRPORT**

CONFESSION

IF GOD EXPECTS ME TO GET INTO A ROOM THAT SMALL WITH A PRIEST, I'M GOING TO NEED A LOT MORE ALTAR WINE.

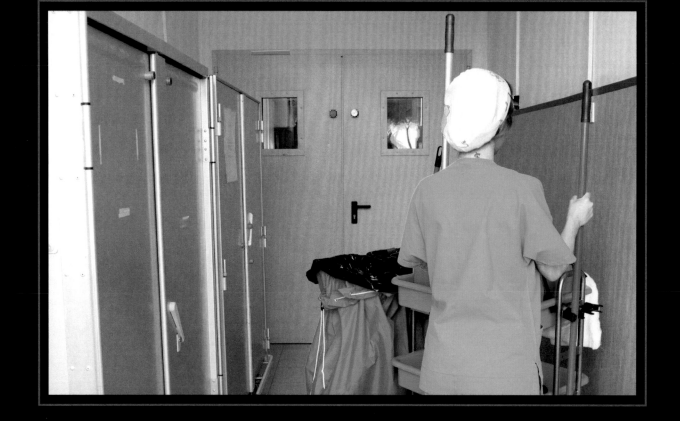

ACHIEVEMENT

CHEER UP, THE WORLD NEEDS JANITORS, TOO.

GIVE IT 110%

. . . You'll Still Probably Come up Short Anyway.

WEALTH

SERIOUSLY, WHAT MORE MOTIVATION DO YOU NEED?

FAMILY

If Life Is a Journey, Family Is a Gift and Children Are a Blessing. . . How Do You Make the Life to Visit Your Gif when the Blessings Won't Even Get in the Damn Car?

REVENGE

**LIVING WELL IS THE BEST REVENGE.
POURING SUGAR IN THEIR GAS TANK IS A CLOSE SECOND.**

ACCOMPLISHMENT

THERE'S NO SUBSTITUTE FOR HARD WORK (EXCEPT BLOWJOBS).

PASSION

**IT STARTS OUT HARMLESSLY,
THEN SOME DOUCHE BAG PAINTS HIS FACE.**

WEDDINGS

YOU'RE GETTING OLD, SHE'S NOTHING NEW, THE SUIT'S BORROWED AND YOUR BALLS WILL SOON BE BLUE.

SOLUTIONS

RUNNING FROM A PROBLEM ONLY INCREASES YOUR DISTANCE FROM THE SOLUTION, UNLESS YOUR PROBLEM INVOLVES KILLER BEES, GRIZZLY BEARS OR AN INDICTMENT FOR YOUR DERIVATIVE TRADING SCHEME

GETTING EVEN

REVENGE IS A DISH BEST SERVED COLD, SO CHECK TO
MAKE SURE THAT JERK WAITER DIDN'T SPIT IN YOUR TIRAMISU.

MISTAKES

THE GREATEST ACHIEVEMENT IS NOT IN NEVER FAILING, BUT IN ALWAYS MAKING IT LOOK LIKE YOU MEANT IT

COPING

WHEN LIFE HANDS YOU LEMONS, SPIKE THE LEMONADE.

ENTREPRENEUR

ON SECOND THOUGHT, YOU'RE MORE THE LOTTERY TYPE.

INFIDELITY

JUST KEEP TELLING YOURSELF IT'S A COINCIDENCE THAT YOUR WIFE'S PERSONAL TRAINER HAS RED HAIR

QUITTING

It Was Probably About Time to Invade a New Country Anyway

WEIGHT LOSS

It Takes Regular Exercise, a Strict Diet and Plenty of Loving Support. On Second Thought, Have You Asked Your Doctor about Lap-band Surgery?

DECEPTION

FOOL ME ONCE, SHAME ON YOU. FOOL ME TWICE, SHAME ON ME. THREE TIMES, WHY DO I KEEP TAKING YOUR CALLS? FOUR, I CAN'T BELIEVE I LISTENED WHEN YOU SAID YOU'D CHANGED. FIVE, "THIS IS TERRY'S WIFE, HE'S NOT ALLOWED TO LEND YOU ANY MORE MONEY."

LIFE

LIVE LIFE LIKE YOU'LL DIE TOMORROW. . .
BECAUSE THE TEST RESULTS ARE IN AND IT DOESN'T LOOK GOOD

GROUP SEX

**NEVER LOSE SIGHT OF THE OTHER GUY,
HE MIGHT BE BEHIND YOU.**

FREEDOM

FREEDOM ISN'T FREE, BUT KEEP AN EYE OUT FOR MEMORIAL DAY MATTRESS SALES

COFFEEHOUSES

MAYBE IF YOU CUT OUT THE FOUR-DOLLAR LATTES

"Couture": It's French for *What the Fuck?*

ARPE DIEN

...Y Is History, Tomorrow's a Mystery, but Today's...

TACTICS

THROW SOME GAMES NOW AND YOU MIGHT STILL END UP ON TOP.

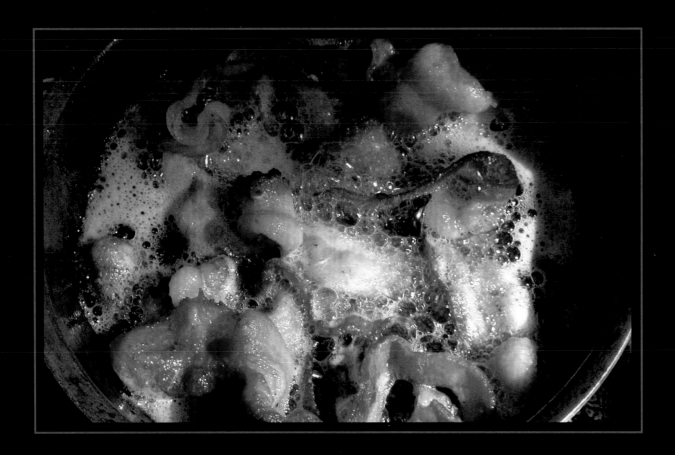

RELIABILITY

**EVEN WHEN YOU'VE LOST THE WILL TO LIVE,
YOU CAN ALWAYS RELY ON YOUR OLD FRIEND BACON.
(WHICH WILL EVENTUALLY KILL YOU ANYWAY.)**

GOATEES

CONGRATULATIONS ON YOUR ABILITY TO GROW JUST ENOUGH
FACIAL HAIR TO MAKE YOU LOOK LIKE A TOOL.

CHARACTER

WATCH YOUR THOUGHTS, THEY BECOME WORDS. WATCH YOUR WORDS, THEY BECOME ACTIONS. WATCH YOUR ACTIONS, THEY BECOME . . . WAIT WHERE WAS I? SCREW IT, I'M WATCHING SOME TV.

INTERNS

BECAUSE EVERYONE ELSE IS TOO GOOD TO MAKE COPIES

MEMORY

**THOSE WHO CANNOT REMEMBER THE PAST ARE CONDEMNED TO REPEAT IT.
THOSE WHO CANNOT REMEMBER ANNIVERSARIES
ARE CONDEMNED TO A NIGHT ON THE COUCH WITHOUT SEX.**

CHARITY

**GIVING TO OTHERS IS AN INVESTMENT IN YOURSELF
(AND A TAX DEDUCTION—GET A RECEIPT).**

PLASTIC SURGERY

EMPIRES

ROME WASN'T BUILT IN A DAY.
THIS MEGASTORE, ON THE OTHER HAND...

FOCUS

SEE PAST THE CHALLENGE. VISUALIZE Y

ONLINE FRIENDS

IF YOU REALLY HAVE 527 FRIENDS, THEN WHY ARE YOU SITTING IN FRONT OF YOUR COMPUTER ALONE ON A SATURDAY NIGHT?

HINDSIGHT

**MAY YOU HAVE THE HINDSIGHT TO KNOW WHERE YOU'VE BEEN,
THE FORESIGHT TO KNOW WHERE YOU'RE GOING
AND THE INSIGHT NOT TO CALL HER WHEN YOU'RE DRUNK**

PERSEVERANCE

**EVERY HOUR SPENT PULLING YOURSELF HIGHER
IS REWARDED WITH AN EXTRA SECOND OF FREE FALL.**

DESTINY

OUR HUSBAND ALWAYS TALKS ABOUT "DESTINY."

MYTHS

Even if It Were True, I'm Still Not Vacationing in Scotland.

MARRIAGE

A DIAMOND'S JUST A PIECE OF COAL THAT DID WELL UNDER PRESSURE. A HUSBAND IS A MAN WHO DIDN'T.

CHALLENGES

THE POWER OF YOUR MIND CAN OVERCOME MANY OBSTACLES. BUT THREE
QUICK BABY STEPS OVER SOME COALS . . . NOT MUCH OF AN OBSTACLE.

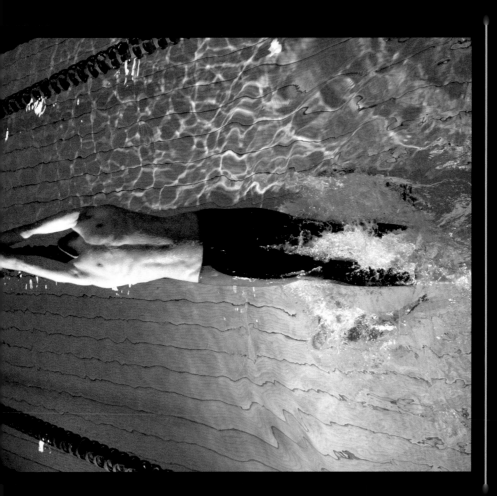

COMPETITION

ALL CHALLENGERS AND RELEASE THE CHAMPION WI

GROWTH

**THERE ARE NO LIMITS TO HUMAN GROWTH . . .
ALTHOUGH 8'11" IS THE ALL-TIME WORLD RECORD.**

EXCUSES

DON'T EVEN BOTHER.

XERCIS

HONOR

SNITCHES GET STITCHES, BITCH.

UNIQUE

YOU ARE ONE-OF-A-KIND, A UNIQUE INDIVIDUAL,
ON YOUR OWN PATH TO THE TOP . . . JUST LIKE EVERYONE ELSE.

CARPOOLING

EVERYONE'S A TREE-HUGGER WHEN IT'LL GET THEM
TO THE GAME FASTER.

WELLNESS

TRENDS

JUST BECAUSE SOMETHING'S POPULAR DOESN'T MAKE IT RIGHT

FORGIVENESS

It's Easier to Beg for Forgiveness Than to Ask for Permission but It's Even Easier to Deny Everything.

VICTORY

. . . FINDS A THOUSAND FATHERS,
BUT DEFEAT IS A MOTHERLESS BASTARD

DIRECTION

WITH DETERMINATION YOU'LL SOAR, SO STEER TOWARD YOUR DREAM
OUGH THE WIND ALLOWS THE HANG GLIDER TO SOAR, AND THOSE T

STONERS

OF COURSE SMOKING POT DOESN'T AFFECT YOUR JOB PERFORMANCE—YOU WORK IN A VIDEO STORE.

EXCESS

STRANGER DANGER

**SHE DOESN'T HAVE ANY TRANSFORMERS AND
SHE IS NOT ON HER WAY TO CANDY MOUNTAIN.**

HATE

TEACHING

THOSE WHO CAN'T DO, TEACH. THOSE WHO CAN'T TEACH COACH THE WRESTLING TEAM.

POVERTY

**GIVE A MAN A FISH AND HE'LL EAT FOR A DAY . . .
GIVE HIM SOME CHANGE AND HE'LL BUY ONE OF THOSE TINY LITTL**
AIRPLANE-SIZED BOTTLES OF BOOZE

ULFILLMENT

LOVE YOUR JOB, YOU'LL NEVER HAVE TO WORK A DAY IN YOUR
(AND EVERYONE THINKS YOU'RE FUCKING ANNOYING).

DEATH

Only Two Things in Life Are Certain—Death and Taxes.
At Least You Can Cheat One of Them Every Year.

GENETICS

SOMETIMES IT'S A BAD HAIR DAY AND SOMETIMES IT'S JUST IN YOUR DNA

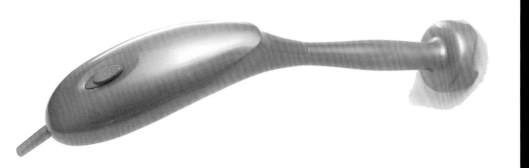

GO FOR IT

**APPROACH BOTH LOVE AND COOKING WITH RECKLESS ABANDON. . .
AND EITHER WAY, THOROUGHLY WASH THE CUCUMBER.**

LAUGHTER

ONLY IS IT THE BEST MEDICINE, IT'S THE ONLY TREATMENT YOUR H
ROVED. SO WATCH TWO *SEINFELDS* AND CALL ME IN THE MORNIN

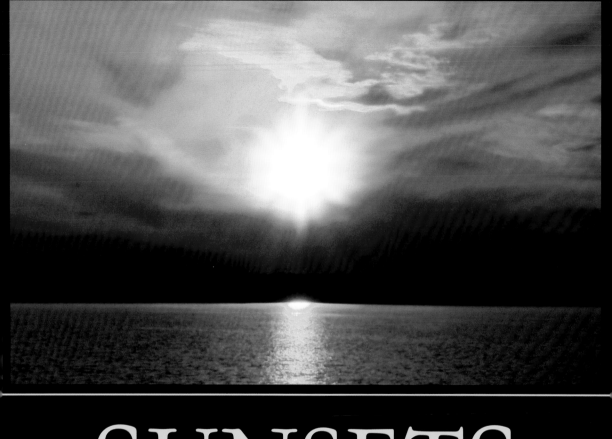

SUNSETS

TRIUMPH

SUCCESS IN LIFE IS NOT MEASURED BY HOW MUCH MONEY YOU MAKE, BUT BY THE MONEY YOU WASTE ON HOT AIR BALLOON RIDES, TANDEM PARACHUTE JUMPS AND BIG-GAME FISHING TRIPS.

BREAKUPS

TIME MAY HEAL ALL WOUNDS, BUT YOUR BIOLOGICAL CLOCK IS TICKING

READING

IT'S EXERCISE FOR THE MIND. SO CONSIDERING YOUR CONDITIONING BETTER JUST TAKE IT EASY TILL THE MOVIE COMES OUT.

SURVIVAL

THE JUNGLE, THE LION MUST WAKE THE EARLIEST, RUN THE FASTEST AND
OUT-HUNT ALL OTHER PREDATORS TO SURVIVE.
SURE MAKES LIVING IN A ZOO SEEM LIKE A PRETTY SWEET DEAL.

SETTLING

WHY LOOK FOR SOMETHING UNIQUE WHEN YOU'RE NOT PARTICULARLY ORIGINAL YOURSELF?

HANG IN THERE

SURE, IT'S YET ANOTHER MONDAY MORNING,
BUT SUICIDES ARE SUCH A BITCH TO CLEAN UP,
AND WHO CAN AFFORD A MAID THESE DAYS?

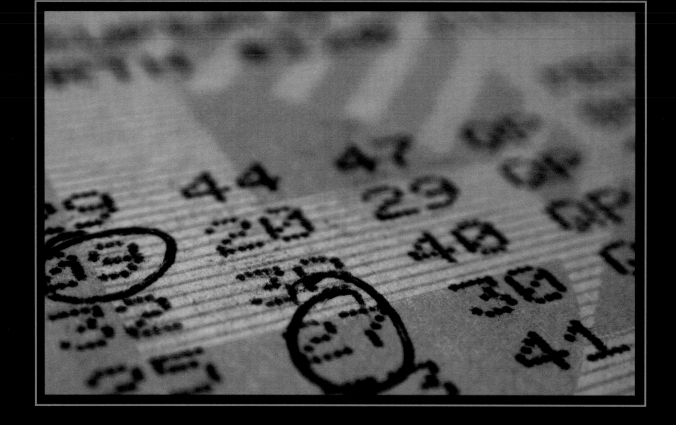

THE LOTTERY

YOU'RE LAZY, LACK AMBITION AND HAVE A TERRIBLE WORK ETHIC, BUT FORTUNATELY THE GOVERNMENT HAS A FOOLPROOF, GET-RICH-QUICK SCHEME JUST RIGHT FOR YOU.

COPS

WORKING YOUR WAY THROUGH A PAINFUL CHILDHOOD ONE TASERED CIVILIAN AT A TIME.

QUALITIE

IT MEANS PERFECTION IN EVERY DETALE, CONSISTANT HARD WORK
AND ALWAYS BEING SHURE TO RUN SPELL-CHECK

BEST FRIEND

He May Always Be There to Give You a High-five but He Still Eats His Own Shit.

WINNING

THERE'S NO "I" IN TEAM. . . BUT THERE IS IN VICTORY, CHAMPIONSHIP AND
WINNING. HOWEVER, THERE IS NO "U" IN ANY OF THOSE WORDS,
SO IN CONCLUSION, MAYBE "YOU" ARE THE PROBLEM.

CHOICES

FISHING

GIVE A MAN A FISH AND HE'LL EAT FOR A DAY.
TEACH A MAN TO FISH AND YOU'LL NEVER HEAR THE END OF IT.

DREAMS

EVERY GOAL STARTS OUT AS A DREAM.
IF YOU DREAM THAT YOU SHOWED UP AT WORK NAKED,
YOU MAY WANT TO REASSESS YOUR GOALS.

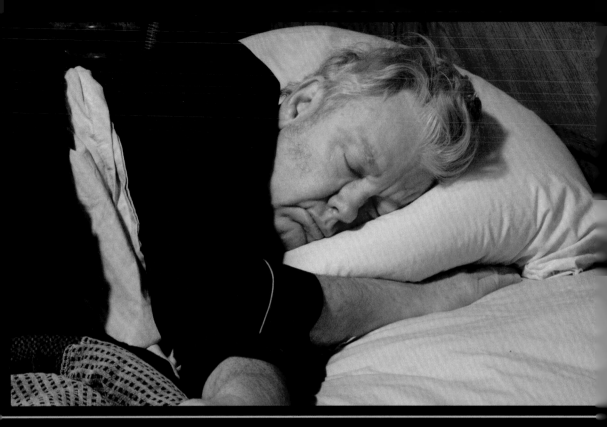

RETIREMENT

THE BEST THING ABOUT RETIREMENT IS WAKING UP EVERY DAY AND KNOWING YOU DON'T HAVE TO GO TO WORK.

DÉJÀVU

It's Not Psychic Premonition, You Just Do the Same Boring Shit All the Time

PROCRASTINATION

DÉJÀ VU

IT'S NOT PSYCHIC PREMONITION,
YOU JUST DO THE SAME BORING SHIT ALL THE TIME

PUBLISHER'S NOTE

PHOTO CREDITS

ABOUT THE AUTHORS

PAUL KOEHORST

Paul Koehorst is a radio, film and TV writer and author living in Los Angeles, California. He is the co-author of *There's No I in Office* and is the artist behind the internationally popular "Sudoku Song." He is available to play golf at your corporate events but only flies business class or higher.

IVOR JONES

Los Angeles resident Ivor Jones was born in a remote town on the southeast coast of Australia in the 1970s. From a young age he was labeled "too weak to farm, too foolish to work" and was shipped to California to enter the entertainment industry. This is his first book of humorous musings.